MAORI CARVING ILLUSTRATED

by

W. J. Phillipps

Author of

Maori Carving, Maori Designs,
Maori Art, Maori Carving for Beginners,
Maori Houses and Food Stores,
Carved Maori Houses and
Maori Life and Custom

with revisions by D. R. Simmons

REED

Contents

Published by Reed Books, a division of Octopus Publishing Group (NZ) Ltd, 39 Rawene Road, Birkenhead, Auckland. Associated companies, branches and representatives throughout the world.

ISBN 0 7900 0116 0

© 1955, W. J. Phillips

First published 1955
Reprinted 1958, 1961, 1966, 1969
Second edition 1972
Reprinted 1973, 1974, 1976
Third edition (fully revised) 1981
Reprinted 1984, 1986, 1989, 1992, 1993

Printed by Kyodo Printing Co., Singapore

1. **Lintel or part of doorway, East Coast style.** *British Museum*

ART THAT IS DIFFERENT

THE CARVING of the Maori people represents the highest artistic achievement. Maori carving is the writing of a people who never needed a written language. All the national conceptions of ancestor respect and allegiance, man's struggle to choose between good and evil, love of children, pride, suffering and defiance are there to be read by the initiated. In these modern days it is often difficult to conceive just what effect or meaning the old-time carver intended to convey. Indeed, many of the meanings of carvings are lost, and it is only in comparatively recent years, during the "carving renaissance" under the late Sir Apirana Ngata, that a knowledge of the carving patterns has been made generally available. However, we are still a long way from a national recognition of Maori carving as the supreme art of New Zealand.

Unlike the rest of the Polynesians, the Maori people preferred curves to straight lines. Only on the Whanganui River did the diamond patterns of Polynesia persist in the carvings of houses and cenotaphs. As in many other departments of life, the Ngati-Porou people, who live north of Gisborne, are said to have excelled in the art of carving; and their carvers often were requested to assist other tribes in the work. Rotorua and Waikato have also produced their great carvers; but these were less widely known among other tribes.

With the advent of European traders and settlers, the use of iron and steel became universal among the Maoris. To some extent an upsurge of carving was the result. Where previously very few carvings existed, large carved houses and monuments to the dead became relatively common. Increased facilities were afforded to expert carvers to journey from home and carry out work for other tribes. The result is that most carvings in museums today are steel tool work of last century. Some were carried out under the instruction of the old tohunga but many others were just copies of yet older pieces. Here and there carvers introduced features not found in really old carvings, but this is rarer than might be supposed. In ancient

2. Arawa carvers at work on house carvings early in the present century. (At left, Anaha Te Rahui; seated right, Tene Waitere.) *National Museum*

times, as now, there were sculptors of exceptional merit as in other activities, and there were also lesser individuals, experts of lower orders who would never emulate the work of the top artists and sculptors. So we may still recognise grades of carving, all of interest, but some more spectacular than others.

Where did Maori carving and design originate? To the casual observer it appears to be different from anything one may see elsewhere. In the amazing manner in which the human figure is presented, the attendant eyed figure, the bold spirals and filling in of spaces, we are offered something which cannot be ignored, an art which claims attention by its own peculiar attributes. We have the choice of two available theories, each of which could adequately explain Maori art and carving in the form which it assumed soon after European settlement. First, there is the theory of an independent origin of

ideas — local evolution of art forms. Given a certain environment, any community of men will settle down and develop an art along definite lines which may be almost identical in many widely sundered places, or may develop along distinctive lines not found elsewhere. Second, we have the suggestion of a diffusion of cultures from a common centre. This is a widely accepted theory which has much to commend it and invites many interesting comparative studies relative to human behaviour. Over the great land masses of the world and even in countries bordering the Pacific there is evidence in support of this theory.

The student of Maori art and carving can decide which of these theories is most likely to be applicable to New Zealand and make comparison accordingly. However, it seems to the writer that while the incoming Polynesians were able to develop a highly specialised wood carving art in this new land, they

4

3. Interior of Te Aomarama, the first Maori carving school established at Rotorua about 1930. *J. W. Chapman Taylor*

4. Carved figures, West Coast, Wellington; akin to old Polynesian types in simplicity of form. *A. Hamilton*

did bring with them an artistic background which influenced their future work and that of their descendants. Each new generation would probably tend to modify or add its own exclusive ideas. Maori carving almost certainly commenced about the time of the great adze and chisel makers of more than 1,000 years ago. Its refinement would come after the discovery of greenstone, not long afterwards. Greenstone, or nephrite, tools had edges that were harder than the later steel adzes. As with the introduction of steel tools, the general use of greenstone tools probably led to a development of the art.

The glories of mountains, rivers, lakes and forests were not for our Maori artist. His art was related to that deep phase of Maori mentality which I have elsewhere termed "ancestor reverence". The Maori did not worship ancestors but he did venerate them very deeply indeed. From them he derived much that made life worth living, his mana or prestige, his rights to land, and his place in society. But apart from all that, there was, and still is, among all Maori people a deep sentimental regard for the dead, who are a living part of the total community. It was this ancestor reverence which produced a Maori carving art where ancestral figures take pride of place.

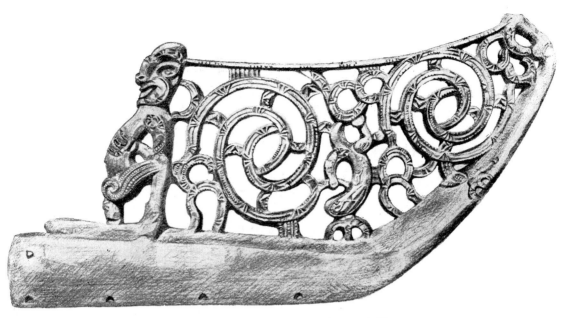

5. Canoe prow from Taranaki. *Margaret A. Morison*

6. War canoe prow seen face on, Poverty Bay style. *National Museum*

7. Enlarged wakahuia end, East Coast style, Norwich Castle Museum. *A. M. Hunter*

THE INFLUENCE OF TAPU

CRUISE, IN HIS *Journal of a Ten Months Residence in New Zealand*, published in 1823, writes of the importance Maoris attached to eating food in the open air, and goes on to mention how the suspension of any article of animal food over the head would be calamitous to those who entered a house. So a dead pigeon or a piece of pork hung from the roof was a better protection from molestation than a sentinel. All this is, of course, related to the tapu of the human head. Even earlier than Cruise was Savage, who published the first detailed account of New Zealand after Cook. This was in 1807. Savage states that between the beams of the ship were nettings filled with potatoes under which Maoris had a great aversion to sitting. He believed this aversion was produced by ideas connected with their religion.

But what is the relationship between the tapu of the human head past or present and the carving art of the Maori? It is that the tapu system of ancient Maoridom was so much a part of life in every department of daily activity that it was carried over into the carver's conceptions of what constituted art. The head, being the tapu part of man in life, must also be the tapu part of man when carved in wood. Maori carvings of the human form are stylised, certainly, but this is seldom at the expense of the head, and throughout the whole field of Maori carving we are impressed with the skill and attention lavished on the head. It is often greatly enlarged and special care is devoted to correct tattoo.

No old-time carver would complete the work of another. Each carving was tapu to its creator. It was in reality part of him, and if he died and another started to work on it, the gods would have their revenge. Loss, suffering, or even death would be the portion of the man who defied tradition and the power of tapu.

Here is a well-authenticated story. About ninety kilometres north of Wellington, near Lake Horowhenua, is a small carved house known as Kikopiri. Ancestral figures line the interior; but the outside carvings were missing for they had been sold in error. This was in 1906. Some years later the tribe determined to replace these carvings, and Te Roera, a trained carver, started to work on a great totara log. He had not progressed far when the mantle of death overshadowed him and the tribe mourned his loss. Years passed. For a long time the people debated the possibility of the new carvings being completed. A young man with some knowledge of carving volunteered to finish the work. All praised the young man and some measures were taken to avert tapu; but, coincidence or not, he died within two years. Nothing daunted, at a later date an Arawa carver came to lift the tapu, and continue the work, but he too died before he could start. So, not far from Kikopiri the log remains till time will reduce it to dust.

In Maori times restrictions of tapu must sometimes have been irksome to men of rank. Truly some were born in tapu, some achieved tapu and some had tapu thrust upon them, but all had to conform to its immutable law. Tapu was "catching" and a man under tapu had to be careful that he did not pass his tapu on to another and so render him a less useful unit in the tribal economy.

We consider here the simple act of drinking water and the precautions which a tapu man had to take. He could not go alone to a stream or river, lie down beside it and drink. He could not take up the water in his hands in case part of his body touched the water and so rendered the stream or river tapu. This would also be the case if he drank water from a calabash — the calabash would be rendered unfit for use by anyone else, and

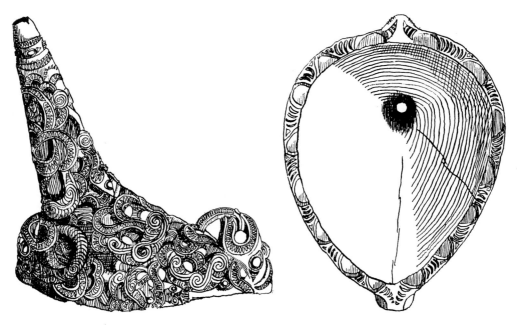

8. Maori drinking funnel. *E. G. White* **9. Looking inside the funnel.** *E. G. White*

even when tapu had been lifted from his own body the calabash could still remain useless.

So the restriction was overcome in a manner well described by Maning in *Old New Zealand*. He writes: "The proper line of conduct for the pakeha in the above case ... would be to lay hold of some vessel containing about two gallons of water (to allow for waste) and hold it up before the native's face; the native would then stoop down and put his hand bent into the shape of a funnel or conductor for the water to his mouth; then, from the height of a foot or so the pakeha would send a cataract of water into the said funnel and continue the shower until the native gave a slight upward nod of the head, which meant 'enough'."

But there was another, and shall we say more refined, way by which tapu men of high birth and breeding might drink, and that was by means of a drinking funnel. I do not think any European has ever seen one of these objects in use. Various authors have referred to them as "feeding funnels". Perhaps food in a state of mulch would be taken in this way, but we are not certain. These drinking funnels must have been very restricted in their locality and in their use and appear to belong chiefly, if not wholly, to North Auckland.

Four beautifully carved drinking funnels are on exhibition in the Maori Hall of the National Museum. These are from the Oldman Collection. All were probably taken to England by early visitors to the Bay of Islands. One of these is well illustrated in Plates 8 and 9.

Mr Rangi Royal, Wellington, says that the tapu of the head is retained more by some families than others. When visiting another town some adopt the expedient of carrying special pillow-slips. There is a story, which has circulated widely in the North Island, of a Maori who married a pakeha wife. On one occasion the wife burned some hair and certain personal belongings of her husband in the kitchen stove. Very soon strange happenings made the house untenable and the family had to depart. Mr Rangi Royal states his belief that it is best to burn hair outside in a special fire well away from food or even the vegetable garden.

TRADITIONAL FEATURES

IN EVERY CARVING ART it seems that something more than the human figure and various volutes are required to satisfy the mind. Something menacing such as a dragon or a snake is usually preferred. The human mind being what it is, harbingers of good are less common. So into Maori carvings has been introduced a manaia, which may be described as a side-faced figure. sometimes humanistic, sometimes bird-like. sometimes like nothing else in the world. Many present-century Maoris whom I have met describe it as an atua (spirit) and leave

it at that. Once it has been pointed out to the student, it is amazing just how many manaia may be seen in a good series of carvings. Heads with an eye and a beak are most in evidence, but a manaia traditionally has something of a body, a leg with three toes, a shoulder, an arm and a three-fingered hand, though rarely are we able to trace all these in one carving.

There is little in Maori art or carving to indicate what some of the earliest manaia looked like, because we have no time scale with which to date our portrayals of this side-face form. However, we will mention three curious types. The first two are found in drawings on rock shelters in Canterbury and the third is from a carved figure on the breast of a burial chest figure from North Auckland and now in the National Museum. These appear in Plates 10, 11, and 12.

10. Lizard-type manaia, Opihi River, Canterbury. *After A. Hamilton*

11. Manaia with three-toed web feet, Opihi River. *After A. Hamilton*

First of all there is a reptilian figure with legs and arms ending in four fingers and a side-turned head in which a large circle may represent an eye, and two small ovals mouth parts. Next is a curious figure with the body ending in a three-toed webbed foot. Attached to its mouth parts is a head which is almost a replica of the first-mentioned reptilian figure. The third figure, drawn from the burial chest, seems to hold an egg in its

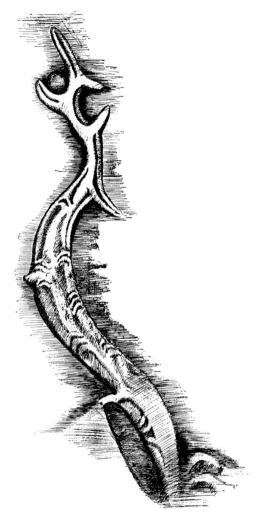

12. Manaia figure on burial chest, Northland. *Diana King*

13. Birdman, Orongo, Easter Island. *After Mrs Routledge, M. W. H.*

mouth, as does one of the figures on the Waverley shelter carvings in the North Island, or is this just a tongue? There appears to be no eye, but just a double mouth with a curious elongated body.

In the Polynesian areas outside New Zealand the side-face figure or manaia is best represented in Easter Island, where a bird-headed man makes its appearance. This remarkable manaia has been cut into the stone by the early masons of that island, using only the most primitive stone tools. In its essential features this figure closely resembles many Maori manaia, but does not always have its three-fingered hand, even though local legend seems to associate it with a bird. (Plate 13.)

However, in Hawaii manaia is known under its own name. In *Who Are the Maoris?* by Alfred K. Newman, we read "They [the Hawaiians] called a bird-headed deity a Manaia, and carved it as a cross-piece on temple doors; but they knew absolutely nothing as to its meaning."

It is remarkable that T. A. Joyce in *South American Archaeology*, 1912, figures a section of a stucco wall decoration from Peru in which about thirty manaia types of the kind seen in Plate 14 make their appearance. This is a bird manaia (though the name manaia is not used in this connection), evidently a deity, for all wear the peculiar "hat", though not all have a dagger shape apparently thrust through the neck. At any rate, here is a form related more nearly to some New Zealand types than is the Easter Island bird-headed figure.

This South American manaia is of interest in that it was probably carved at a period of anything up to 2,000 years ago. It is a bird with a wing, an arm with a three-fingered hand, a leg ending in three digits and a tail of similar type. Did early Polynesian voy-

14. Design on stucco wall, Peru. *After T. A. Joyce, L. L. Buswell*

15. Draconian monster, Peru. *After T. A. Joyce*

agers visit Peru and influence their art, or did South Americans voyage, or drift on their rafts, far over the Pacific bringing the manaia to widely sundered lands? Alternatively, there may once have been a centre of dispersal somewhere in the Pacific, from which a form such as this originated, and where now it is absent. For comparative purposes one of the toothed side-face figures from South America, with a small koru over the middle of its head, is depicted in Plate 15.

A study of a bird-man type of manaia in New Zealand is illustrated in a pendant of pale greenstone from Oparure, Te Kuiti. This remarkable pendant has been well photographed for us by Charles Hale. (Plate 16.) It was purchased for the National Museum from Mr K. E. Williamson. This manaia has a convoluted body and human characters. The type of body belongs to North Auckland and western districts of the North Island as far south as Taranaki. The object is 6.19 cm long and 3.8 cm wide below. Above, a crest appears, and below it is the suspension hole. A well-formed beak bends downwards to meet the breast. The eye appears incomplete. The body is U shaped, humanised below after the manner of a Maori tiki, with feet in apposition. An arm, strongly made, emerges below the shoulder and bends downwards in typical fashion to grasp the body below with a large three-fingered hand.

16. Bird-type manaia pendant. *Chas. Hale*

MARAKIHAU

IN THE BAY OF PLENTY district the legends of deep-sea taniwha and ocean gods became crystallised in a figure known as marakihau. (Plate 17.) In the late 19th and 20th centuries this figure has acquired attributes from European legends of mermaids. Marakihau has become an established feature of a number of Maori houses throughout New Zealand and even male and female figures are recognised by modern carvers. The oldest photograph of a marakihau of which we have any record was taken with a group of old carvings about the period 1865–80 and illustrates a female. A feature of many of these marakihau is the crown on top of the head — an enlargement of tara tara o kai, the side-cut notch, but which here may be derived from pakeha contact (see p. 23.)

However, it seems certain that marakihau as a mythical sea monster entered into Bay of Plenty legends beyond the time of European contact. This denizen of the deep was said to have a human form and in addition a long tubular tongue termed ngongo. Through these long tongues the monsters could draw down and swallow canoes and men on the surface. Elsdon Best relates that "several stories are on record in which the Maori claims that certain ancestors of his were, after death, transformed into marakihau."

Two marakihau carved in traditional style appear on the porch of the carved house at Te Kuiti. This house, dating from about 1875, was carved for Te Kooti and is among the finest in the North Island. Carvers from the Bay of Plenty assisted in its erection. In 1887 a house was built for Te Kooti at Martinborough, some of the carvers employed being familiar with the marakihau on the house at Te Kuiti. So marakihau appeared on the porchway of this house, which unfortunately was burnt down in 1933. From an old photograph an artist has made the drawing of the type of marakihau used in that house.

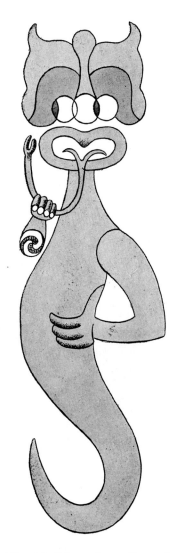

17. **Marakihau, Martinborough carved house.** *Ray McKay*

13

18. An early photograph of a marakihau, left. The tara tara o kai carving is used on the head and side of the body. *National Museum*

THE ONE-EYED FIGURE

HERE AND THERE among old carvings there is presented a human face with only one eye. (Plates 19 and 20.) This one-eyed figure is found on old burial chests of North Auckland as well as in Taranaki and Wanganui. Even a soapstone bird call, evidently from the South Island, shows this feature, for which no satisfactory explanation is forthcoming.

There are various local legends of one-eyed monsters such as a strange being of old, part god, part man and part fish, who had only one human side to his face and had but one eye and one arm. This demi-god could live equally well on land and in the sea. This story was told by James Cowan as the Arawa explanation of manaia, but it could equally refer to a single-eyed being. Also at Taupo, there was a remarkable being who lived in the deep water of the lake. His body was said to have been washed up on the shore, when the single eye was seen.

The two illustrations of this feature show first a typical Northland head, pointed above and narrow across the eyes, removed from its context of volutes and contortions on a

20. Taumata atua with blind eye, Taranaki. *L.L.D.B.*

19. Northland head, from "Torino", K. A. Webster collection. *L.L.D.B.*

wooden flute or putorino, now in the K. A. Webster collection in the National Museum; and second a wooden peg-like shrine (god stick) used in Taranaki to hold the essence of a spirit god. The remarkable convolutions which represent arms, legs, and body in this amazing object are worth study.

THE THREE-FINGERED HAND

THE THREE-FINGERED hand is a feature of most old carved figures, and a number of ingenious legends have arisen to account for it. Sometimes the three fingers are accompanied by a thumb also, and sometimes two fingers and a thumb are used. Again, as in certain of the old burial chests from North Auckland, researchers find the human figure with the three haohao (skeleton fingers) while the feet have the three webbed claws of a water-bird.

Now, from *Maori Carving*, 1941, we repeat some explanations of the three-fingered hand.

Graham, in *Journal of the Polynesian Society* (Volume 30, p. 253, 1921) states: "Pere-tu had only three fingers: this was not a deformity, but a sign of his descent from a reptile god ancestor. Thus it is that carved effigies of ancestors are shown with three fingers, as a tuhi (sign) that such were men of god-like descent, though they themselves may have had hands like ordinary mortals.

In *The Maoris of New Zealand*, 1909, James Cowan states: "The first man of the Maori race to carve and decorate houses as we carve them today, was Nuku-wai-teko or Mutu-wai-teko, or, as some tribes have it, a man of Hawaiki. He had only three fingers on each hand, and he perpetuated this in his carvings. All his figures he carved with only three fingers on each hand, and this has been kept up even to this day by Maori carvers. This was in the very remote past when the ancestors of the Maori lived in the islands beyond the Moana nui a Kiwa."

T. Herberley, formerly Maori carver at the National Mueum, always believed that Tiki (said in some legends to be the first man) had three fingers and, being taxed on the

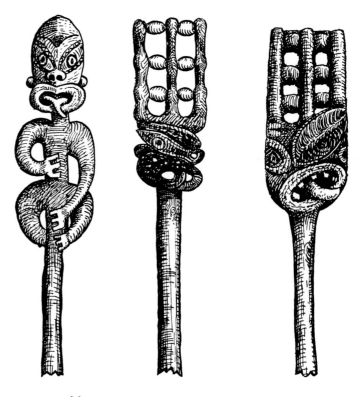

21. Designs carved on the upper ends of ko or digging sticks. Here is demonstrated the use of the complete human figure or teko-teko, and the three-fingered hand with manaia heads below. These heads are of the closed-mouth type. *After Best. Sketch, Miss E. Richardson*

16

22. An unusual carved figure, Te Arawa territory. *Auckland Museum*

question, showed what he could do in the carving of human figures, all of which had three fingers.

An interesting explanation was given to me by Hare Hongi (Ngapuhi Tribe). It appears that when held correctly, the sacred rubbing-stick or *hika* used in fire generation is controlled by only three fingers. The three-fingered hand thus becomes a reality during a process which for the Maori had such a high significance.

East Coast tradition maintains that Hingangaroa was the first carver. He had three sons, Taua, Mahaki and Hauiti. These sons established themselves at points on the coast and spread the knowledge of carving. From these three sons arises a story that is the East Coast explanation of the three-fingered hand.

In the *Maori Record* (Feb. 1st, 1907, p. 71), Professor Macmillan Brown summarises the results of his inquiries in the Urewera.

23. Carving of Whakatohea tribe, Opotiki – a pre-European wall slab from a chief's house. *Chas. Hale*

24. Tekoteko, gable ornament in Gisborne style from Weraroa Pa, Taranaki, 1865. *Auckland Museum*

25. A carved, hatted figure. Note the large hands. Arawa carving. *National Museum*

Two old carvers held that five fingers made the figures "too human", and that it was tapu to represent the true human figure in carving. Ancestors were spirits or gods, and features must be obscured. A four-fingered figure represented an ancestor of the European era.

However, the late Elsdon Best took the wider view. The late Mr T. W. Downes, Whanganui, inquired from him his opinion of the three-fingered hand and received in reply a postcard which is, to say the least, expressive. Here it is:

Three fingers — as old as the grey hills. Throughout the wide world the three-fingered hand appears in ancient works — on European tombs, Japanese sculptures, in Peru, etc. It was a Chinese ideograph for Man. On ancient carvings of Greece and India. Fatima's hand placed over Mahommedan doors to ward off evil had three fingers. On ancient sculptures of Nineveh are the three *haohao*, seen on Maori grotesque figures. Too old — origin lost. No man knoweth it; for who shall get behind Nineveh?

18th August, 1924.   Elsdon Best.

Apart from any consideration of the fact that fingers usually number three, we are aware that fingers form an outstanding feature of Maori carving. This is particularly the case in many of the older types of carved figures. No matter how complicated the design, one can usually see eyes, arms and fingers, and next to eyes it seems that fingers most readily claim attention.

26. War canoe prow, South Taranaki carving. *Copenhagen Museum*

SPIRALS

MAORI SPIRALS are a fascinating subject for study. Most of them are double, that is, two volutes swing around in parallel fashion to meet or coalesce in the centre. Very often the total number of volutes is considerably increased, the carver's object being no doubt to bewilder the uninitiated and increase the beauty of his production. This study of spirals may be opened with consideration of a single element, a curving stalk with a bulb at one end. As a simple decoration this may be seen in Plate 27 on a slate breast pendant of Poly-

nesian form from Shag Point in Otago. The curving stalk or koru is best known as the basic element of the black, white and red Maori rafter patterns. Like the three-fingered hand, it has a world-wide range, and it appears most unlikely that this form originated in New Zealand.

There are a number of instances of the koru being used as a spiral, or stages in which spirals appear to have a relationship to the conception of a koru. These need not have any significance in the evolution of spiral forms but they are of interest to the student.

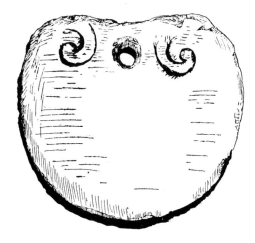

27. Slate breast ornament, Shag Point, Otago. *S. Traill*

28. Boundary stone spiral, Opunake. *J. Brennan*

29. Double koru spiral on stone sinker, Nelson. *L.L.D.B.*

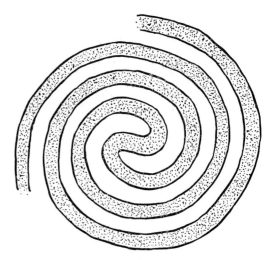

30. S-curve spiral from the same sinker. *L.L.D.B.*

A koru spiral may be seen in Plate 28. This is on a boundary stone near Opunake, Taranaki. Plate 29 is drawn from a carved stone sinker picked up in 1865 at Brightwater, Nelson. In this later instance the artist has made two arms to his koru spiral. The simple koru spiral is the famous volute found on the capitals of Ionic columns, but is much older than that, being also almost worldwide among primitive peoples of Asia and America. Consideration of the koru spiral cannot be left without reference to a canoe bailer from Banks Peninsula in Canterbury Museum (Plate 31). A rafter pattern design occupies the lower centre and a small double koru spiral appears on the extreme right. Note the modern koru spiral of the background, so like old Maori types.

This brings the present study to the more common types of Maori spiral, an S-curve type, a spiral that partially interlocks and an interlocking type. Plate 30, also drawn from the stone sinker from Brightwater, illustrates a simple S-curve type as seen in the shaded portions. However, it will be seen that the white background consists of two partially interlocking arms; so both these types are nearly always seen together. On this basis, also, even a single spiral has its background which makes it appear to have another spiral interlocking with it. Plates 33, 34, and 35,

31. Canoe bailer from Banks Peninsula. *G. Hillsdon*

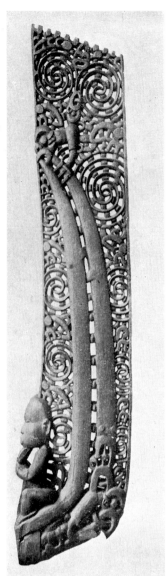

32. Stern post or taurapa of war canoe, Wanganui. *After Best*

drawn by the author, show a hypothetical
series constructed to show how any native
people who commonly used the koru in carving would soon arrive at fundamental spiral
types. Even though some of these intermedi-
ate stages have been recorded in old Maori
carvings, I am not prepared to state that any
particular one of the double spirals originated in New Zealand.

In Plate 32 the upper manaia figure is
known as paikea, while the figure at its base
is Tawhirimatea, lord of the tempest.

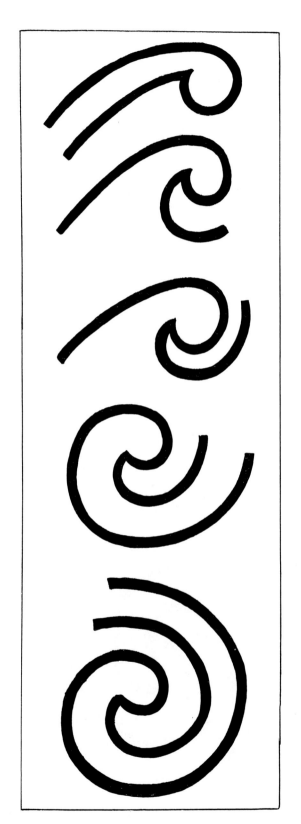

33. The koru in relation to spirals. *W.J.P.*

21

34. The koru in relation to the interlocking spiral. *W.J.P.*

35. The koru in relation to the S-curve spiral. *W.J.P.*

36. A nguru flute in the Oldman collection. *Gordon White*

DECORATIVE FEATURES

MAORI CARVING has developed from a point where only the head and certain parts of the body were adorned with carving to the modern era when blank spaces are rare and every part must be profusely decorated. This profusion of decoration is certainly found in old wooden articles; but this is not common on large pieces, probably on account of the limited facilities of the carver. The filling-in of spaces has always been an important feature of Maori carving, and sometimes objects are completely covered with this filling-in technique. A nose flute from the Oldman collection illustrated here well demonstrates this point (Plate 36). Here the eyes are a central recognisable feature but for the rest the decorative carving consists of carving elements inside of which are running scrolls or rows of notches.

Decorative work in which notched ridges run parallel to one, two, or three plain ridges is termed rauponga. Plain ridges are known as patapata, and the hollows between ridges are haehae, while the notched ridge itself is termed pakati. Individual notches are arapata. Once these terms are memorised the rest is easy. In general, the East Coast of the North Island formerly used a three-sided notch or arapata in the pakati, while Rotorua

and the Bay of Plenty developed a four-sided notch. In Taranaki carving it is possible to find not only both these types but also chevron and diamond types of notching in the pakati. The chevron type is also found in some Urewera carvings in the National Museum; so the position is a little unsatisfactory, and it is not always easy to state the locality of a carving from a study of pakati. A carved panel from Te Hau ki Turanga well portrays the use of rauponga (Plate 38).

From the use of a ridge of raised notches the survey passes to a type of carving in which notches are cut sideways to give a ridge with a zigzag notching running along each side. This is the East Cape method found on the Te Kaha storehouse in Auckland Museum. A later variation of this pattern is found in the Bay of Plenty and sometimes in the East Coast around Poverty Bay. Usually there is a plain ridge in the centre between the notches. As will be seen, this is the old water-symbol which has an almost world-wide distribution. An old East Coast stockade post seen in Plate 37 has been used to exemplify this type of carving, which is called by the euphonious name of tara tara o kai — literally, peaks and peaks of food. As might be expected with such a name, tara tara o kai

23

carving is almost universally used on carved food storehouses or pataka. It varies somewhat and not all tara tara o kai is broken up after the manner shown on the stockade post.

Unaunahi is the term used by Anaha te Rahui of Rotorua to refer to the type of carving ornamentation in which crescents appear in grooves, sometimes in rows, and sometimes in groups of three or four. The term unaunahi refers to fish scales; but as crescents appear carved on digging sticks, a crescent origin is in the meantime presumed. On the Whanganui river, the term ritorito is applied to unaunahi when used in groups of three. In the hands of Poverty Bay carvers, the crescents have been utilised to produce some of the beautiful and artistic figures which adorn the carved house in the National Museum. The unaunahi design is the most difficult to carve correctly, and has been comparatively little used by carvers of the past century. A good example of this class of work is seen on the maripi or shark tooth knife depicted in Plate 46.

At the heading of this chapter is depicted a nose flute from the Oldman collection of Polynesian artifacts in the National Museum. Here again may be seen the blind-eye conception, with rauponga of a single notched row enclosed in plain ridges. The other eye is surrounded with a running scroll design known as pakura.

The use of spirals with partially interlocking ridges is a feature of this design. These particular spirals have always seemed to me to symbolise the restraint of the carver and to be older than the spirals with ridges completely interlocking.

The stockade post shown on this page and already mentioned is one of the unique figures of its kind. It portrays the perfect water symbol which in pataka carving can become very involved indeed. The broken arms probably once held a taiaha or spear. It should be noted here also that on one shoulder use has been made by the carver of a partially interlocking spiral.

37. A stockade post near Wairoa. *J. McDonald*

38. A carved slab from the carved house in the National Museum. *National Museum*

39. A carved lizard from Rotorua. *J. McDonald*

THE LIZARD

BECAUSE only one animal, the lizard, is faithfully depicted in Maori carving, it is worth more than passing mention. Possibly most of these are carvings of the tuatara. In studies on Otago middens in days before the First World War, the writer made a small collection of tuatara lower jaws. These were taken among all sorts of kitchen refuse — bones, shells, oven stones, charred sticks, and the like.

So there seems to be no doubt but that in Otago, at least, large numbers of tuatara were eaten in former days.

Here is a tuatara story from Dr. H. D. Skinner, then Director of the Otago Museum. It was told to him about 1900 by Willie Grey, Stony River district, Taranaki, a well-known identity among the Maoris of that district last century. Maori people of Taranaki recog-

nised that at one time the tuatara was eaten by the people, for the tale as told by Willie Grey was that in days of old a man went out to collect tuatara for the oven and brought back a basketful. Instead of handing them over to the woman who had charge of the cooking, the man threw the basketful of tuatara on the fire. His action evidently became historical. It would be a studied insult to the woman and help to deprive her of mana.

Why the lizard should be so reverenced as never to be distorted none at this late date can say for certain. We do know that the small green lizard was feared beyond all animals in the forest. Probably remembrance of the crocodile in a far-off tropical home and the dread which it inspired was transferred to the smaller lizards. The personified form of the common green lizard is

40. Sketch of a green tree lizard. *J. Buchanan*

26

41. A lizard entering the mouth of a carved figure, Rotorua. *J. McDonald*

Rakaiora, who is viewed as atua or god (Plate 40).

In New Guinea, crocodile and snake names coincide with lizard and eel designations current in many Pacific dialects. The natives of Yap have a horror of eel, and never eat it. The Mortlock Islanders call the eel Tiki-tol and use it for the equivalent of the Serpent in the Garden of Eden. The Maori version is that sin came into the world because the eel tempted the first woman. Would we not expect to find some indication of so important a legend in Maori carvings?

The following story was given to the writer by A. C. Christophers, Rotorua: "The chief, Ngararanui, was a descendant of Whakaue of Te Arawa. He is always depicted in carving as having a lizard going into his mouth. When he was young he travelled to Waikato and eloped with a beautiful girl of that tribe. Together they arrived at Rotorua; but the girl was not long contented with her new home, and back the couple returned to Waikato. In claiming forgiveness, she exhibited her husband to Waikato and boasted that there was no feat he could not accomplish. After consultation, Waikato chiefs placed a large lizard in front of Ngararanui, daring him to eat it. This the chief reluctantly did, so he was named Ngararanui, and his fame has not lessened to this day." (Plate 41.)

An interesting fable bears on this point. The shark wished the lizard to go with him so that both might become denizens of the ocean. The latter objected to leaving the land, whereupon the shark said, "Very well, you stay on land and be loathed by men." Replied the tuatara, "It is well, for that is one of my powers. But you will be caught by a hook, and your head will be battered by a root pounder, after which you will be hung up and dried." Both of these things have come to pass, for the lizard is a fearsome creature in the eyes of man, while all know that the shark is caught, killed and dried by man to serve as food.

NGUTUIHE

WHEN A GREAT CHIEF died it was customary to erect in his memory some form of monument or cenotaph. This memorial carving was often the canoe of the chief, cut in two, and upended with the prow pointing upwards. The upper portion of a small canoe cenotaph in the National Museum is seen in Plate 42. Here the reader must turn the book upside down to study the type of face portrayed. It will be seen that this figure is remarkable in having the upper lip prolonged to an inordinate degree, fitting in nicely with the space to be carved. This type of figure is termed ngutuihe, literally, a beak or lip resembling a garfish. This ngutuihe figure is found here and there in carving, and in rare instances the beak is shown coiled. In general, also, it may be that the selection of a canoe as a memorial has some relationship to the journey across water which the soul of the departed must make after death. In many lands of the old world the canoe has been used to symbolise this journey.

A ngutuihe figure, remarkable as being the only one of its kind, is in the National Museum (Plate 43). It comes from a pa stockade near Nuhaka on the East Coast. This figure is identical in shape with the elephant god (Ganesa) of India and Java. A well-educated Indian recently looked at this pa post on view in the National Museum and assured those with him that he "worshipped that god". Dr Newman in *Who are the Maoris?* was the first to point out this similarity. However, in this ngutuihe figure the presence of teeth on each side of the prolonged upper must be noted. The barred appearance at the back of the mouth could

symbolise gills, for many curious beings of Maori mythology are credited with an aqueous existence. It cannot by any means be stated as certain that this figure is derived from the elephant god of India and Java though the possibility exists, and all ngutuihe may be similarly derived.

The relationship of ngutuihe to manaia cannot be overlooked. Many manaia are seen with a prolongation of the upper part of the beak (or lip) and in such cases the lower part of the beak often becomes folded upwards underneath the upper. This feature may be studied in Plate 68, which illustrates the centre board of a tuere of a canoe. In the National Museum, the terminal manaia of the main pataka on exhibition in the Maori hall as well as other pataka carvings illustrate this prolongation of the upper beak or lip. These are all the work of Te Arawa or Bay of Plenty carvers. It may be mentioned here that most of Te Arawa carving has been largely influenced by carvers of the Ngati Pikiao tribe, Bay of Plenty, who claim close kinship to Te Arawa.

A series of sample carvings prepared by Anaha Te Rahui for Augustus Hamilton about 1905 are described in *Maori Carving* (1941). Here the manaia as illustrated by a carved slab has both jaws equal; but in another type of manaia, which Anaha terms ngututa, the upper lip is definitely stronger than the lower. This strengthening of the upper jaw without making it appear much longer than the lower is also a feature of the National Museum carving of a pa gateway or waharoa.

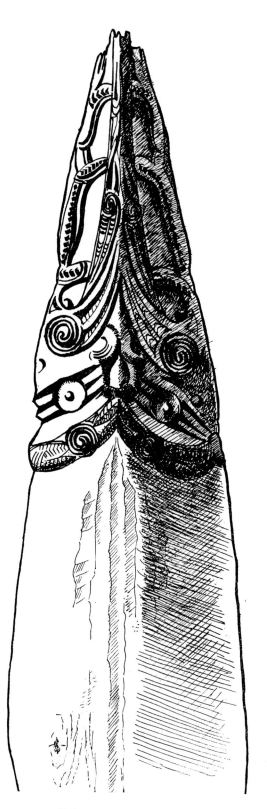

42. A canoe cenotaph. *L.L.D.B.*

43. A stockade post, East Coast. *National Museum*

44. Taiaha combat, as demonstrated at the Christchurch Exhibition, 1906, by Doctors Wi Repa and Peter Buck (Te Rangi Hiroa). *A. Hamilton*

CARVING ON WEAPONS AND TOOLS

THE MAORI carried his carving art over to many articles of everyday use, implements of agriculture, fowling, and fishing, and also to weapons of war. The taiaha, a slender weapon usually made from manuka, and measuring from 1.5–2m in length, was regarded by many great orators as indispensable when delivering a speech on the plaza or marae in front of the assembly house. In fighting, the blade was well polished, and much care and attention was given to the adroit feints and passes necessary to overcome an adversary. The point was much used to poke an opponent about the centre of the body, and so, when an adversary was off guard for a moment, the blade was swung into action. The taiaha points as seen in Plate 45 are of much interest in that they disclose how the Maori carver has ingeniously enlarged the human tongue so that its defiance

reaches even to the enemy. Above the tongue are forehead, eyes and upper lip.

When Maori gatherings were held, young men were put through their paces in the art of war. This was continued into this century, when some of the older warriors were still alive. An accompanying illustration shows two young medical doctors, Peter Buck and Tutere Wi Repa, at Christchurch Exhibition, 1906-7. They are being initiated into the use of taiaha and are at the ready position (Plate 44).

Tools and implements for everyday use were adorned with carving according to the importance of their owners and the amount of carving talent available. This feature is clearly shown in three shark tooth knives or maripi with wooden handles (Plate 46). The maripi is a superior type of cutting implement used in North Island localities

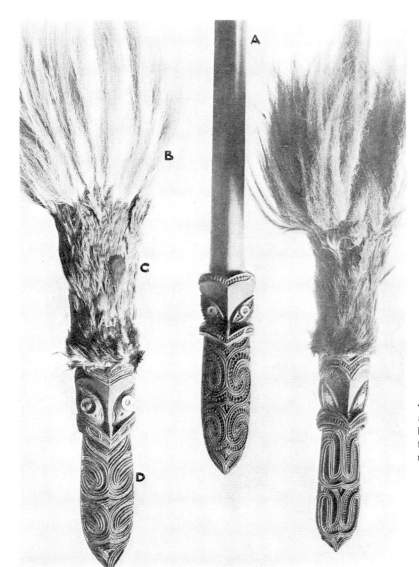

45. Taiaha points: Taiaha kura (left and right). A, blade or rau; B, white hair, awe, of native dog; C, red feather sheath, Tauri kura; D, tongue or arero. *National Museum*

where teeth of the seven-gilled shark are available for use in the wooden handle into which they are securely glued and sewn. Here we have a tool with a well-defined handle and an enlarged body, the teeth being attached to its convex edge. It is probable that when not in use these cutting tools would be suspended as they were objects of some tapu, being used only to cut up human flesh. This is evidenced by the cord or thong attached to each.

The maripi on the right is blocked out or shaped for the detailed carving of a semi-human form. It was collected by Captain Cook. It is painted red and black. Perhaps at this stage it was urgently required for cutting meat and was never fully carved, or perhaps the carver died before it was completed and no other would finish the work. The central maripi illustrates the work of one of the lesser carving schools. This is the type of carving too often said to be due to European influence; but the conception of rauponga unaunahi and the waharua (or diamond shape) carving is Whanganui. The four-fingered hand may be a relic of certain west

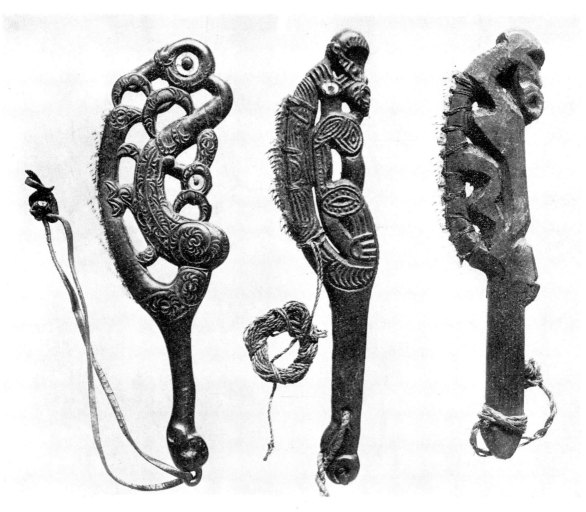

46. Flesh-cutting knives, British Museum. *British Museum*

coast, North Island carvers who preferred to use four or five fingers. The peculiar feature of a stout arm running upwards to end in four fingers on the neck is seen in this work. A manaia face is formed by the use of a paua shell ring or tiwha inserted below the fingers.

On the left is an ornate maripi of superior style, and from the fact that the carver made use of a single three-toed foot of a type seen also on old burial chests from Northland it is inferred this item came from that area. With its attenuated body and double beak

the manaia assumes a menacing posture. Secondary work is in unaunahi. Two large crescent forms are seen on the upper part of the manaia body. These may symbolise feet. It is probable that a knife such as this would be most highly regarded by its owners. With successive generations of users it would become highly tapu, chiefly on account of the veneration attached to the dead who had handled it. In all, the carving is exquisitely presented and its general style seems to indicate a pre-European manufacture.

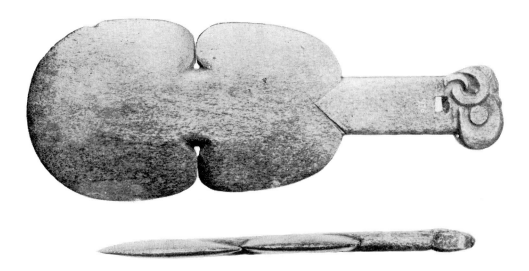

47. Short lobate bone weapon, Kotiate. *National Museum*

48. An ornate carved wooden weapon, Wahaika, of the 19th century, made in Poverty Bay. *A. Hamilton*

49. Bone Wahaika, valued weapons. *National Museum*

WAKAHUIA

AMONG OBJECTS which have survived from the stone-carving period of Maori culture are a number of papahou or wakahuia, boxes to hold small treasures such as prized feathers of the huia, amulets, pendants and necklaces. Most papahou were well carved and much treasured, being handed down from one generation to another. A halo of tapu surrounded them because of the ancient treasures they may have contained, particularly combs and feathers once worn on the heads of ancestors. A papahou carved in the Hokianga style of North Auckland is illustrated in Plate 50. No fewer than four human figures may be traced on the lid, two of these upside down, their legs and arms being symbolised by entwining eel designs composed of single ridges of pakati. Some of these pataki ridges take on a figure-of-eight appearance. Paua eyes are encircled here and there by entwining eel shapes. The whole effect is indicative of a high order of artistry. This papahou is in the British Museum.

In recent years an interesting experiment has been conducted by Mr J. M. McEwen, formerly Secretary of Maori Affairs. Using a few greenstone tools borrowed from the National Museum collection, he was able to carve a papahou (or wakahuia) of which a photograph is here reproduced (Plate 51). Mr McEwen selected a piece of totara and set to work, taking as his model a photograph of one of the wakahuia in Peabody Museum, Salem, Massachusetts, collected in the Bay of Islands in 1807. Unfortunately, he did not have a chisel narrow enough to get much depth, but found that by carving with greenstone tools it was not very difficult. The greenstone chisel could perform as well as a steel chisel, except that it took longer to accomplish the work. Also, the greenstone chisel retained a good edge and did not need continuous resharpening.

Previously, Mr McEwen had experimented using small, more or less oblong greenstone chisels held in the hand, and found that, with patience and application to the task in hand, it was possible to block out and carve in the details on a typical Maori head in a relatively short time. He tells us that "following on this experiment, and after many years of practical experience in Maori carving, I have come to the conclusion that there is no certain method of determining by examination whether a particular example of Maori carving has been done with stone tools or with primitive steel tools . . . seasoned totara is the ideal wood for carving; but if it is seasoned to such an extent that the sap has completely disappeared and the wood lost its resilience, the result will be pitted surfaces and rolled edges in spite of the quality of the chisel or the skill of the carver."

50. Treasure box, British Museum. *British Museum*

51. Treasure box or papahou. *Chas. Hale*

35

52. Kaitaia carving, Auckland Museum. *Auckland Museum*

EARLY CARVING

NEW ZEALAND'S great ethnologist, the late Elsdon Best, always believed that certain unusual carvings from swamps and caves in North Auckland were the work of the early Maori. It may well be that Elsdon Best was right in his belief, and many of these carvings should be regarded as the prototypes of the more highly ornate examples of later years. A selection of these carvings, all now in Auckland Museum, is here supplied.

Features of these carvings are a more simple approach to the portrayal of the human figure, the use of side-cut triangular notches which in certain instances are used to depict teeth, the use of a chevron and a single spiral instead of a double one. There is present also the raised or shaped eyes with no suggestion of paua shell ever having been inserted. It is in the far north or in the far south of New Zealand that one would expect to find the old features which the later Maori

would have in the main discarded. These are the marginal areas remote from main centres of culture and development.

In the first instance a group of three chests collected from Whangaroa comes to notice. These are relatively much smaller than other bone chests from this area and may possibly have once served to hold the bones of children or parts of skeletons as did that on the right. As in most Maori carvings, the importance of the human head is emphasised. All have raised eyes, but in the first figure in Plate 54 there is the peculiar feature of a tear. In the other figures the teeth are large and triangular, while upturned legs support the jaw. Fingers or toes are the normal number and on the ill-formed thighs a single spiral appears. In Plate 54 the head and body are one, supported by legs which join the upper portion of the peg-base.

The Kaitaia lintel is another carving re-

53. Canoe prow from Doubtless Bay. *Auckland Museum*

36

lated to this early group and to many lintels of apparently much later date. Essential motifs are a central human figure with a filling-in of chevrons and out-facing manaia at each end, though in this instance the manaia appears to symbolise a lizard. This may be one of the early manaia prototypes, and if so could account for the presence of teeth in later developments of manaia. It is true that a manaia with teeth would be more satisfying to the ancient artist than one without. The human figure has the head well formed, but low on the body, reminding us of certain Whanganui carvings. One writer has noted how this position of the head and the hands partly outspread is related to figures carved on a god-house in German New Guinea.

Related to the Kaitaia lintel is a canoe prow from a swamp at Doubtless Bay. Here again manaia appear; but in the main figure the mouth is closed with large triangular teeth inside and some projecting points sur-rounding the head and neck. Other carvings from the far north also show this feature outside the figure. Turning our attention to the Chatham Islands, we find that the natives there used a bird form in place of manaia. This was also notched on the outside. The notched figures are also recognised by Dr R. S. Duff in his book, *The Moa Hunter Period of Maori Culture*, 1950.

In continuation of this early pre-Maori series study turns to a small bone pendant from Nelson (Plate 55) which illustrates a type of face quite unlike later Maori work. It is also notched around the outside edges. The use of three plain grooves to represent eyes is quite unusual. Lips are pouted and notched and a tongue is evident, while the nose is realistic. The whole appearance is downcast and angular below. In fact, its maker has achieved an appearance foreign to our usual conception of the face in Maori carving, but not unknown in island Polynesia.

54. Bone chests from a cave at Hokianga. *Auckland Museum*

55. Bone pendant, Nelson. *J. T. Salmon*

37

ARAWA CARVING

A STOCKADE or pa post from Te Arawa territory appears in Plate 57. Here is the hatted figure so typical of carving of that area, a large head, once tattooed in thorough and exact fashion, small oblong mouth, eyes apparently closed and hands in a position favoured by carvers of that region. This may be a representation of that illustrious first eponymic ancestor, Tiki. All pa posts seem to have symbolised Tiki from whom, say some, all men are descended.

A popular account of the origin of man relates that the brother of the great Tane, Tumatauenga, decided that instead of gods, man should inhabit the earth. On Papa, the mother earth, he formed an image in his own likeness, and this he placed at a tuahu, a hillock of earth in which were placed two green branches, symbolising life and death. Then, by means of rites and his own marvellous powers, he endowed the image with life. This first living person of the male sex was Tiki.

An old carved figure in Copenhagen Museum may be part of a pa post or one of the stockade figures from a pa (Plate 58). The head is unusually large and the body uncarved, a feature being the large three-fingered hands. The head is hatted, and the tattoo is well featured. On the whole the face is much more realistic than is usual among carvings of this nature. Large hands of this kind are a characteristic of many old carvings and are a reminder of the importance which appears formerly to have been given to the hands as a decorative element in the representation of the human form. The one element which does not appear to harmonise with the rest is the diamond in the centre of the forehead, which may be of later date.

A carving in the National Museum (Plate 56) illustrates the perfection with which the Maori artisan could portray the human head when he wished to do so. Two heads of men, beautifully tattooed, are to be seen in this plate, illustrating the use of the koru in the adornment of the forehead and chin. Below is a well-modelled head of a woman. Again it is evident that the koru is the most important feature of her tattoo. The eyes of the woman are closed and her head inclines to one side. Two manaia are to be seen, one on either side. Their beaks seem to bite the upper portion of the head. This carving was produced in 1896 by Tene Waitere for Augustus Hamilton of the National Museum.

56. A unique carving in the National Museum. *National Museum*

58. Carved figure in the Royal Danish Museum, Copenhagen.
Sophus Bengtsson

57. Hatted figure, Rotorua vicinity.
National Museum

59. Assembly House, whare ruanga, Te Kuiti, 1899. Carved and painted in Mataatua style about 1875. *National Museum*

CARVED HOUSES

THE ASSEMBLY HOUSE or whare runanga is often well adorned with carvings. It is the focal centre for village life and here all important functions take place. Such large houses developed in the mid-19th century with steel tools. The earliest example still intact is the house in the National Museum, carved in 1842 by Rukupo at Manutuke, near Gisborne in Poverty Bay. In construction, there is a central ridge pole which is said to symbolise the back bone of the ancestor after whom the house is named, and from this ridge pole the various rafters descend. The ridge pole is upheld by end poles and one or more central poles. Rafters are supported below by upright slabs, poupou, which are often carved.

The house itself is usually named after an ancestor of the tribe, and all carved figures have some intimate association with the local people or their associates, though great ancestors such as Maui, Kupe, Kahungungu and Tama te Kapua may also appear.

In the illustration above is a frontal view of the large assembly house at Te Kuiti named Te Tokanganui-a-Noho. Here is a wide and open porch with a central pou tahu or ridge pole support in front, and on the back porch wall a door and a window. Above the pou tahu at the apex of the barge boards is a single carved head with double tongue. Below, the barge boards fit behind the upright, outfacing amo. Usually a threshold board or paepae limits the porch area in

40

60. Amo, Mataatua. *Sophus Bengtsson*

61. Carved doorway, Whanganui. *G. L. Adkin*

front. In modern houses it is higher than here depicted and is usually carved.

In several old carved houses dating well back into last century it was noted that many of the carved slabs have a plain base and were buried some little distance in the ground. Two amo (side upright carvings on superior houses) now in the Royal Danish Museum, Copenhagen, illustrate this feature and are uncarved and rounded below (Plate 60). These slabs are of Mataatua workmanship, the upper figures being typical koruru with rounded eyes and the lower figures wheku with slanting eyes. The Mataatua carvers sometimes cross their feet as in the upper figures but the lower figures with feet in juxtaposition are quite typical. This latter feature is typical of the greenstone tiki. One unique feature of these carvings is the fact that in one a single figure holds a mere in its three-

41

62. Carved ancestral figures around inside walls of National Museum whare runanga. *National Publicity Studios*

fingered hands; but in all other figures no hands appear. In fact it would almost seem that the carver had produced a series of figures with hands behind their backs.

The doorway is well carved with a lintel or pare above and is supported by uprights on each side. Certain pare on modern houses are of considerable age, for these as well as certain other carvings are said to be handed down from one house to another. At the back of the porch and inside the building they are preserved from the weather, and so the student of today can study old carvings in most unexpected places.

The interior of the carved house is well illustrated in Plate 62, where the carved slabs which line the walls are shown with rafters fitting down above. This remarkable house is known to have been carved in 1842–43 under the direction of one of the great carving tohunga of Poverty Bay, Raharuhi Rukupo. The standard of workmanship is very high indeed. The visitor to the National Museum is able to study in detail this house erected in the main Maori hall.

It is not usual to see carved figures on the lower rafter ends, and this is perhaps a distinctive feature used on special occasions.

Between the carved slabs are panel spaces filled with decorative lattice work known as tukutuku. The designs from left to right are roimata toroa (albatross tears); patiki (flounder); waharua (double mouth); kaokao (ribs, armpits), and on the back wall whetu (stars) or roimata (tears) and another waharua.

EAST COAST CARVING

Araised carved knob in the centre of the forehead may connect certain Maori carved figures with old wooden carved figures of India. But in the East Coast it is said the knob represents the handle of a paddle with the design appropriate to the owner. The feature is often to be seen on East Coast figures. Two house carvings from this area illustrated in Plates 63 and 64 exhibit the carved knob. One is known by a photograph among a series collected by the late Augustus Hamilton about the end of last century which is now in the Auckland Museum. This figure belongs to the old Poverty

63. Carved Figure, East Coast. *A. Hamilton*

64. East Coast figure in the Ethnology Museum, Berlin. *W. R. B. Oliver*

Bay school of carving, though the use of four fingers and the less well-formed unaunahi could place it in a later carving school. It was found at Whangara, and is a wall slab of a house which belonged to Hinematioro, a

66. Koruru from the East Coast. Tongue with hollow for inser-tion of paua eye. *National Museum*

65. Koruru, probably cut from prepared plank, East Coast.
National Museum

well-known chieftainess who lived in pre-pakeha days.

The second specimen, now in Berlin, is re-markable in that a dancing figure may be seen on the body beneath the tip of the tongue. This dancing figure was perhaps once an important element of old Maori art-istry. It may be traced in house carvings from Waikato to Wellington and can even be seen in the Chatham Islands, but seems largely to have disappeared elsewhere. On the west coast of the North Island it is said to be associ-ated with a bird, and was called kaeaea. The

Berlin carving is also notable for the use of unique spiral types on shoulders and hips. They are carved in tara tara o kai.

The two koruru figured above are East Coast types, which can sometimes be ident-ified by a triangular notching in the pakati. In the above figures we note identical fea-tures in the use of a forehead knob, ears sym-bolised by spirals, the presence of teeth, and tongues out-thrust. I have been told that orig-inally the ridge pole was continuous with the koruru which was carved at its outer end in a vertical position. Certain National Mu-seum carvings seem to bear out this state-ment. 'A "neck" behind the head would hold the weight of the maihi (gable facing boards).

67. Maori war canoe, Gisborne. *After Cook*

CANOES

CAPTAIN COOK'S illustration of a war canoe portrays one of the most impressive pictures of its kind ever made. A fully equipped war canoe, in this case carrying at least fifty-four warriors, must have been a most picturesque sight. Feathers of the hawk were used to adorn both prow and stern, apparently symbolising the qualities of that bird.

The large and prominent spirals seen on most war canoe prows and depicted clearly in the illustrations on this page[1] and on page 19 are of the type known as takarangi. Here the pakati is separated into groups which hold the plain ridges in position. This is one of the spiral types where the plain ridges completely interlock. A somewhat broken prow (Plate 26) now in Copenhagen Museum illustrates this spiral type. The frontal figure often has the tongue out-thrust, and the forehead is high and somewhat crested above. The eyes are of the wheku type, that

is, they are set in slanting sockets.

Some of the most beautiful carving known is to be seen on the prows and stern posts of Maori war canoes, this being particularly so with the northern or Waikato type. This type of prow is known as tuere. Below the tuere at the extremity of the bow is a single carved head usually termed parata. This parata is sometimes chinless to offer less resistance to wave action. The central board of the tuere is constructed with a number of strengthening ribs running from below upwards. These are usually rounded at the sides and made into eel-like manaia with heads above. The tuere in the British Museum, London, which is here figured (Plate 68) is remarkable for the excellence of the running scroll design or pakura with which it is adorned. A little below the apex are two manaia with interlocking mouths and the same is evident near the upper posterior margin. Below are forms used in strengthening the whole. On these the eel-like manaia rests, though curling tails below may be the ends of bodies. One of the beasts has the head of a man while the other has a manaia head.

[1] The spirals shown on this war canoe were probably incorrectly drawn by the artist for Maori spirals were double and not single in form.

68. A northern-type prow or tuere. The original is in the British Museum. *National Publicity Studios*

In Plate 5 is depicted another tuere type of prow from Taranaki with interlocking spirals adorned with groups of unaunahi. Between the large spirals is outlined a manaia figure while another figure at the prow has the head missing. Looking into the canoe is a large figure of unusual design. The whole centre board is here actually a part of the heavily made base which fits on to the canoe as a haumi or bow cover.

Plate 32 is a detailed view of the stern post of a war canoe. It may be noted that the stern post is fortified against wave action by means of a double rib running upwards along much of its length to end on its inner edge where it is grasped by the three-fingered hand of a manaia or enters its mouth. As already stated, this manaia is known as paikea, while the figure at its base is tawhirimatea, the lord of the tempest.

46

69. The late master carver John Te Kaure Taiapa (left) and the former director of the school of carving at Whakarewarewa, Mr Kuru Waaka. *National Publicity Studios*

70. Lectern (1972) for the Mairehau High School, Christchurch.

THE MODERN CRAFTSMEN

AT THE NEW ZEALAND Maori Arts and Crafts Institute in Rotorua the ancient art of Maori wood-carving in its traditional forms is taught to the youth of today. The institute was created by Act of Parliament in 1963 for just this purpose, for the preservation of all forms of Maori arts, crafts and culture which were so rapidly disappearing before the influence of European civilisation, Christianity and industrialisation. Carving, the prestigious art of the Maori people, takes pride of place in the work of the institute.

The institute could not have made a better choice for its master-carver than John Te Kaure Taiapa who, with his celebrated brother Pine, were themselves pupils of the old masters and had been responsible for the erection and renovation of innumerable Maori meeting-houses throughout the country. The present master carver is Tony Tukaokao, noted house and canoe carver.

Apprentices whose ages range between fifteen and eighteen years are taken on a three-year apprenticeship course and paid according to the Carpenters' and Joiners' Apprenticeship Award rates. Their basic training is carried out on large carvings for meeting-houses, work orders for which are being continuously received by the institute. In order to diversify, the apprentices are taught the production of souvenirs for which there is a continuous demand, especially from overseas tourists who may see the artifacts actually being produced.

The institute is often criticised for its attitude of adopting traditional execution of carving, as in some quarters it is considered that an art would die if it were not allowed to change into other art forms, but the institute maintains that successful departure from conventional rules and traditional styles requires firstly a sound knowledge of them.

71. Canoe stern post, carved for the New Zealand Embassy in Bangkok, Thailand. *National Publicity Studios*

All over New Zealand are Maoris in many walks of life who have either had carving experience or have some knowledge of it. It is an art that will continue into the future and become adapted to modern conditions as required. The old-time experts have trodden the well-beaten track to the setting sun; but a younger generation takes up their work with new hope and new inspiration.

72. Poupou for the Rotorua International Hotel (the paua eyes have not yet been inserted).

48